# Scream Machines

## Roller Coasters Past, Present and Future

### Herma Silverstein

Walker and Company
New York

*The author would like to thank Ron Toomer, chief engineer of the Arrow/Huss Corporation, for his time and patience in teaching me how to build a roller coaster; the members of the American Coaster Enthusiasts who so generously provided photographs for this book; and the many United States historical societies for helping me locate roller coaster facts and photographs, and for referring me to others in the field.*

First published in the United States of America in 1986 by the Walker Publishing Company, Inc.

Published simultaneously in Canada by John Wiley & Sons Canada, Limited, Rexdale, Ontario

Library of Congress Cataloging-in-Publication Data

Silverstein, Herma.
  Scream machines.

  Includes index.
  Summary: Discusses roller coasters, their origins, history, revival in popularity through theme parks, and possible future. Includes a list of America's best roller coasters.
  1. Roller coasters—History—Juvenile literature.
  2. Roller coasters—United States—History—Juvenile literature.
  [1. Roller coasters]  I. Title.
GV1860.R64S57  1986      791'.06'8      86-1554
ISBN 0-8027-6618-8
ISBN 0-8027-6619-6 (lib. bdg.)

Designed by Laurie McBarnette

Printed in the United States of America

10 9 8 7 6 5 4 3 2 1

# *Contents*

*To Sue Alexander, Eve Bunting, Terry Dunnahoo, and Jane Yolen for their constant encouragement through all of the ups and downs of the ride. And to M.F.G., who knows why.*

*The Python of Florida's Busch Gardens.*

# Introduction

Snap! The switch is thrown. You dig your finger-nails deep into the leather harness as it locks against your chest.

Five, Four . . .

Too late to back out now. Hold your breath.

Three, Two, One. Wham!

You are catapulted out of the station, the speed of your car going from zero to fifty-five miles per hour in four seconds. Your heart beats wildly.

Screaming, you race up a length of track, then top-ple over, upside down and around a 360-degree loop!

Your heart's in your stomach, your stomach's in your feet as powerful gravity forces grab you and pull down hard. You scream louder, fearing you'll go right through the bottom of the car. An instant later, the car darts out of the loop and tears down the track, lifting you out of the seat. You begin to breathe again, when all at once you realize you're headed up a dead-

*The Colossus of Magic Mountain Park, California.*

end hill, four stories high and you're not stopping. You're about to fall off the cliff . . . when the car comes to a sudden stop.

Hanging suspended on the tracks, gravity disappears, leaving you totally weightless, for a second. Then the car begins falling backward.

You want to scream, but this time the wind steals your voice. Speeding, the car falls down, then up, then goes upside-down and around the loop in a terrifying backward flip. Once out of the loop, you discover you are going up, feetfirst, to the edge of yet another dead-end hill!

Seconds before being vaulted into space, the car stops. You hang weightless at a right angle to the ground, when, surprise, you're falling headfirst! You leave your heart at the top . . . the ground's a blur . . . and finally you *scream,* and race back to earth and safety.

You have just experienced a ride on one of the very latest roller coasters. This scream machine, with its tubular steel tracks, catapulting launch, and backward somersaulting loop is space age in design and thrills. Yet its origin comes, as do all roller coasters, from one basic emotion—sliding down hills is fun!

*A typical 17th century Ice Slide.*

# 1

# *In the Beginning There Were Ice Slides*

If you had lived in Russia in the 1600s, you could have sped down the first "roller coasters" ever in-vented—giant slides covered with ice. These "ice slides," as the rides were known as, were a popular winter sport in Russia for over two hundred years.

The slides stood seventy feet tall and were supported by a strong wooden framework. Russia's freezing winters made manufacturing ice for the slides an easy task. An attendant simply poured water down the ramp, which quickly froze into a slippery sheet of ice. A sled ride down an ice slide would have been at lightning speeds.

But even before the ride, there was a thrill in store for you. In order to reach the launching platform, you had to climb a seventy-foot ladder at the back of the slide. Once on top you would choose one of the special guides employed to accompany riders down the ramp. The guide would sit on a sled, two feet wide

*The 1817 Bellevue Mountains featured two towers where boarding took place.*

and one foot long. Then you would sit in the guide's lap.

When the "coast" was clear, the guide would scoot the sled to the edge of the platform and give it a shove. Down the ramp you would shoot, covering the distance in a flash. Following this, the sled would race across a six-hundred-foot-long straightaway, gradually losing speed until it came to a stop at the base of another ice slide. This second ice slide was identical to the first, except it faced in the opposite direction.

You and your guide would get off the sled and carry it while you climbed to the top of the second ice slide. Then you would repeat the ride, "coasting" in the opposite direction, to end up at your original starting point, the base of the first ice slide.

Ice sliding was enjoyed by all economic classes in

Russia. Slides were built in large cities, small villages, and in the private gardens of wealthy citizens. Royalty also enjoyed the sport. The ice slides near St. Petersburg were strung with colored lanterns along the straightaways, making night sliding not only an exciting sport, but a beautiful one too. The rides were so popular that in 1754 Empress Elizabeth sponsored a carnival just for ice sliding.

Despite their obvious success, it took until the early 1800s before the idea of ice slides spread beyond Russia. It was then that a traveling Frenchman, whose name has been lost to historians, visited Russia and took a ride on an ice slide. He was so impressed with the amusement that he decided to introduce ice sliding into France. But there was one flaw in his clever plan—the warm French climate kept melting the ice!

Fortunately, the Frenchman did not give up at this point. He merely adapted the Russian winter sport into one for summertime. He built a hill made out of timber and installed wide rollers down the center. Sleds with runners on the bottoms coasted down the rollers similar to the way baggage coasts down modern conveyor belts, and at about the same slow speed.

Not much in white-knuckle thrills, but when the Frenchman installed his ride at a popular picnic garden, his ride proved a hit and the "roller coaster" was officially born. French inventors and engineers soon realized that roller rides were a money-making opportunity, and several versions of this roller coaster began to appear at other picnic gardens in France.

The first true scream machine, named the Russian Mountains after its ancestor, was built in 1804 in the Ternes section of Paris. Tracks replaced the wide rollers. And instead of sleds, small one-passenger carriages with wheels on the bottoms were used.

The switch from rollers to wheels was a giant step forward in roller coaster design. The layout of the Russian Mountains, however, seemed to leap backward in time. The ramp was erected so high off the ground that on take off the car plunged into a sharp dip. Safety belts had not been invented, so passengers frequently fell out. When riders did manage to complete the circuit, they faced a long, steep climb back up the incline for a second turn.

This "hiking" drawback was remedied in 1817 when another primitive coaster, named the Bellevue Mountains, was installed in a Paris suburb. As with the Russian ice slides, the Bellevue Mountains was constructed with two inclines facing each other across a straightaway. However, the only climbing necessary was a trek up a towerlike structure in order to board. Additional climbing was eliminated because the carts raced down the first ramp so fast that the force of gravity kept the carts speeding over the straightaway and *up* the second ramp before stopping. In order to return to their original starting point, passengers simply repeated the ride in reverse.

A few months later, further advancements were seen with the premiere of the first racing coaster named the Promenades Aeriennes, or "Aerial Walk." The ride consisted of two cars each holding two passengers. The cars took off at the same time and followed separate tracks. After the initial downward trip, the cars curved around the banked turn at the far ends of the tracks and raced back up their separate inclines into the station. The use of circular tracks, combined with

*The Promenades Aeriennes or "Aerial Walk" was the first racing coaster.*

the force of gravity, provided the cars with enough momentum to keep them going until they had reached their original starting points.

Another plus for the Promenades Aeriennes was permitting riders to buy several tickets at once. Riders could pass one to an attendant each time their car crossed the finish line, which did away with the bother of getting out and waiting in line for another time.

The Aerial Walk caused such a sensation that people came to the amusement park just to watch it in operation. A Paris newspaper of the time ran an article describing the daredevil ride. "The passengers take their places in four elegant cars and reach the height of eighty feet, running at a speed equal to that of a galloping horse. Then they come down, then up again, and so on, until they are back at the starting point, from which they can start on another journey, and travel at forty miles per hour. This is as fast as the fearless aeronaut travels through space in his balloon."

The article went on to describe the ride's features, including a guide rail on both sides of the tracks which prevented the cars from "jumping." Engineers cautioned attendants to keep the tracks clear of all debris, pointing out that a "passenger once lost a leg due to the presence on the track of a horse chestnut, which upset the car."

The chance of injury did not seem to deter riders, or those determined to improve the rides. Monsieur Lebonjer made getting on roller coasters much more pleasurable when he patented a lifting device in 1826. He designed a cable mechanism that pulled the coaster cars and passengers up a steep ramp, after which the cars sped down the other side of the ramp by gravity. Riders no longer had to climb a tower to get to their car.

Fortunately, in contrast to most French roller coaster inventors who took out patents at this time, Monsieur Lebonjer actually built his invention. Because of the way Monsieur Lebonjer's lifting device worked, the terms "lift hill" (the first incline up which the cars are hauled) and "first drop" (the plunge down the lift hill) were adopted into roller coaster terminology. In addition, Monsieur Lebonjer's cable device became the basis for future, more advanced lifting mechanisms.

In 1848 French engineer Monsieur Clavieras heightened the thrills when he opened the world's first looping coaster, the Centrifugal Pleasure Railway at the Frascati Gardens.

*The Centrifugal Pleasure Railway was the world's first looping coaster.*

"Today has been tested the only existing Chemin du Centrifuge we have in France," an article in the *Journal du Havre* stated proudly. "The starting point is thirty feet above the ground, and the one hundred and five foot slope drops seventeen feet every three and one-half minutes. The terrific speed at which the cars enter the loop (more than one hundred and fifty miles per hour) was especially noted."

After this trial run, in which sand bags substituted for passengers and did not fall out, a French workman volunteered to ride the looper. Onlookers were so worried that a collection was taken up for the man's family in case his upside down ride ended prematurely. The *Journal du Havre* continued its coverage of the historic event by saying the workman "had no trouble breathing, and during the loop experienced such a delicious feeling that he wanted to try again."

Regrettably the courageous worker's name was never recorded, nor is there any evidence of whether this coaster was built as a legitimate ride, or merely as an entertaining demonstration.

After this period of amazing roller coaster development, the French, for no apparent reason, lost interest in the ride. Coaster mania would not revive again until the end of the nineteenth century, when ride inventors in the United States, thanks to an abandoned coal mine and some intrepid mules, finally caught the fever and started building all-American scream machines.

# 2
# *Coasters Cross the Atlantic*

The year is 1843 and you're sitting in an open coal car, on top of Sharp Mountain, Pennsylvania. You stare past the passengers standing in the car ahead of you and peer down the chillingly steep slope of the mountain. The engine chug-a-chugs, and the train begins to descend.

The wheels clang over the tracks, slowly at first, then faster and faster as gravity takes control and you plunge down. The passengers in the car ahead of you let out a loud, "Aa—eee—haw." Trees whiz past and the ground looks like a blurry green carpet being pulled out from under you. Careening over a hilly bump, the wheels fly off the tracks for an instant, sending you flying up, then crashing back down into your seat.

The cars veer to the right, then the left, aiming for the bottom of the mountain, and straight toward a canal! Your screams compete with the clang of the wheels and the chug of the runaway train.

*The mules may be gone but the Mauch Chunk Railway rolls along.*

Then at the last moment, gravity loses its power, and the train roars to a stop, brakes screeching, cars shaking, engine puffing. Your knees wobble as you climb out of the coal car. The other passengers are led out of theirs, braying. You have just ridden the Mauch Chunk Switchback, America's earliest known "roller coaster." The passengers riding in the car ahead of you are mules.

Yes, as strange as that seems, America's first roller coaster riders were mules. Originally the Mauch Chunk Switchback was a coal mining train that carried coal from the mine on top of Sharp Mountain down to the village of Mauch Chunk. The engine was needed to get the heavy line of cars moving downhill initially and to stop them at the bottom. The mules were given a "free ride" in railway cars built especially for them. Since the engine had no gears for reverse, it was the mules' job to haul the empty cars and the engine back up the mountain for another load.

By 1870 the coal mine had spread over a larger area of the mountain and the switchback route was abandoned. Fortunately for future roller coaster lovers, the tracks did not lay idle. The citizens of Mauch Chunk decided to use the deserted mine train for sightseeing and called it the Mauch Chunk Switchback Railway. The lifting device was a steam engine located on top of the mountain, which wound two steel cables around a metal drum. A ratchet rail laid between the tracks prevented the cars from slipping back down. Once at the top, the cables were unfastened, and the cars coasted to the bottom of the mountain. Passengers paid five cents to ride at the rather tame speed of six miles per hour. Despite its lack of thrills, the Mauch Chunk Switchback became so popular that for many years the Pennsylvania railroads ran special trains to the area so people from all over Pennsylvania could experience the new pleasure ride.

The success of the Mauch Chunk Switchback spawned other versions called "artificial coasting courses," or "artificial sliding hills." These spin-offs resembled the primitive French coasters in that they had short, inclined runways with wide rollers placed close together down the middle. Sleds with runners coasted down the rollers by gravity. Even though wheels eventually replaced the rollers, Americans coined the name for these rides which endured—roller coasters!

Artificial coasting courses formed the main attraction at the pleasure resorts which sprang up throughout America during the 1870s. Just as happened in France, several ride inventors took out patents for their roller coaster designs.

One of the first patents was issued to Richard Knudson of Brooklyn in 1878. His proposed ride consisted of a thirty-foot vertical elevator at each end of a double, parallel track. Knudson's cars held four passengers, seated two to a side facing each other. This meant that two riders would go down the track backward every time.

One elevator would haul the car and its passengers to the top of the incline where it would coast to the bottom. Then the second elevator would hoist the car up to the other, parallel track, and riders would coast in the opposite direction to their original starting point. Knudson's idea was workable, but his plan went the

17

way of many would-be roller coaster inventors of the era—into the wastebasket. Richard Knudson never built his ride.

One American coaster inventor did manage to get his plans off the drawing board in 1884. La Marcus Adna Thompson had been inventing things since he was twelve years old, including a rotary butter churn. He also built carts for his friends and an ox-wagon for his father. It seemed only natural that he try his hand at inventing a pleasure ride such as the Mauch Chunk.

Thompson decided to install his roller coaster at Coney Island, a beach resort in Brooklyn, because it was the largest such area in the country. His friends predicted that his ride would never succeed, but Thompson went ahead anyway and unveiled his creation on June 13, 1884.

Named Thompson's Switchback Gravity Pleasure Railway, the roller coaster consisted of two boarding stations, one at the top of a double, parallel track. The cars held ten passengers each and coasted at six miles per hour down the gently sloping four-hundred-fifty-foot track. At the bottom, riders would get out and follow as two attendants pushed the empty car up the incline to the second boarding station, then switched it onto the parallel track. The passengers would re-board and sail back in the opposite direction to their original starting point.

Although Thompson charged five cents a ride, his doubting friends were speechless when they learned his daily receipts totalled seven hundred dollars. Thompson recovered his original investment within three weeks. Such success was noticed immediately

*La Marcus A. Thompson would eventually construct forty-four coasters in America and Europe, earning the nickname of "Father of Gravity."*

*Richard Knudsen's coaster patent shows his lifting device for cars.*

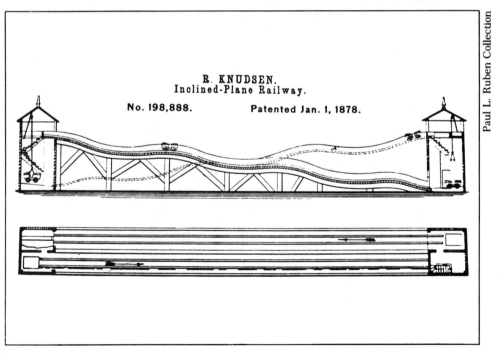

**R. KNUDSEN.**
Inclined-Plane Railway.

No. 198,888.      Patented Jan. 1, 1878.

19

by the owners of picnic gardens, and they quickly filled Thompson's mailbox with orders for Switchbacks. By 1888 he had built twenty coasters in America and twenty-four in Europe, earning the nickname of "Father of Gravity."

Less than a year after the opening of Thompson's Switchback, other ride inventors journeyed to Coney Island to try out their own coaster ideas. Charles Alcoke's Serpentine Railway solved a problem no other American coaster inventor had been able to do: return riders nonstop to their original starting point. Alcoke built his track in an oval shape, which is the way practically all roller coasters have been built ever since. In sending the cars *out* over the tracks and *back* again, the oval track acquired the name "out and backs." The six-passenger cars on Alcoke's Serpentine looked like park benches, and riders sat sideways, enjoying the scenery as the car glided around the track at a brisk fifteen miles per hour.

*Frank Leslie's Weekly* said the ride "is a contrivance designed to give passengers all the sensation of being carried away by a cyclone. . . ."

In 1885 another ride inventor, Phillip Hinckle of San Francisco, arrived at Coney Island. Hinckle turned riders around by placing his coaster seats to face forward in his Gravity Pleasure Road. He used a steam-powered chain lift to haul the cars up the first incline, variations of which have been used on practically every coaster since. Once the coaster reached the top of the lift hill, the chain releases the cars, and they coast downhill by gravity alone.

Phillip Hinckle's chain lift convinced other ride inventors that they had to make coasters more thrilling for passengers, and easier to operate for attendants. Hinckle, however, lacking a progressive personality, retired from the coaster business after the success of his first, and only, roller coaster.

In the meantime, La Marcus Thompson was losing money on his Gravity Pleasure Railway, mainly because Alcoke's and Hinckle's roller coasters were more modern. Thompson decided to fight back by building the "ultimate" roller coaster. First he improved upon the best features of his competitors' rides, then added a few ideas of his own.

For starters, he invented the automatic cable grip, the first roller coaster safety device. The cable grip was attached to the bottoms of the coaster cars. Automatically it grasped or released the lift-hill cable whenever the cars rolled over a trigger placed at strategic points along the track. Thus, if the coaster stopped for an emergency in the middle of the ride, the cable grips prevented the cars from rolling back down the track.

Next, Thompson revolutionized the design of coaster cars themselves. By joining two long cars, he formed the first roller coaster train in history, while at the same time doubling the number of passengers able to go around the tracks from six to twelve.

La Marcus Thompson did not stop with mechanical improvements. He also invented visual effects to go with his "ultimate" coaster. He put a tunnel over the tracks, the sudden darkness adding an element of danger to the ride. As the train went through the tunnel, the cars tripped a switch which flooded the surroundings with the latest novelty of the day, the newly invented electric light. Scenes of the Orient

Dragon Gorg
Revere Beac

The Dragon Gorge Scenic Railway was a typical turn-of-the-century coaster.
This one included a pavilion to house the coaster, as well as a restaurant
and souvenir shop.

23

were painted on the walls, and riders enjoyed viewing the mysterious murals. Thompson named his creation the Oriental Scenic Railway and unveiled it in 1887 at Atlantic City, to rave reviews. Thompson's advertisement slogan was "Ride It Just for Fun," which became his slogan for all his scenic railways.

La Marcus Thompson was now besieged with orders for scenic railways so he formed his own company, the L.A. Thompson Scenic Railway Company. This type of roller coaster was housed inside a large building called a pavillion. The pavillion also had a soda fountain, restaurant, and souvenir shop so thrill-seekers could entertain themselves while waiting to ride the roller coaster.

Even with their elaborate new features, scenic railways remained primitive rides. They were shaped so much like commercial railways that commentators marveled at how people paid for amusements which resembled aspects of their daily lives. One journalist noted, "the switchbacks and scenic railways are merely trolley cars, a little more uneven in roadbed, jerky in motion, and cramped in the seat than the ordinary means of transportation, but not much."

If coaster owners wanted to give the public a ride they would dash back in line to ride again and again, designers would have to do more than put a car on a slight incline. Future roller coaster inventors would have to create architectural extravaganzas on wheels.

# 3

# Turn-of-the-Century Thrill-Hills

The great enthusiasm for America's pioneer roller coasters awakened fearsome fantasies in coaster inventors throughout the United States. Enterprising showmen took out patents for longer, higher, faster "scenic railways."

One of the most daring of these designers was J.F. Meyer. Meyer wanted to give a blast to riders by shooting them out of a cannon at the top of the lift hill. His Leap the Gap roller coaster would then jump across a six-foot-wide gap, high off the ground, and land on tracks at the other side. Then the Gap would speed back to the loading station.

As improbable as this sounds, Meyer was able to construct and successfully test his ride at Coney Island in 1902. Empty cars were used for the test, which established a fixed weight for the train. This allowed Meyer to calculate the speed of the train in advance to insure that it would make it across the gap. He knew, however, that when passengers rode in the cars, the weight of the train would change for each ride, thus changing the trajectory, or the path, of the leap. Meyer's solution was to have passengers "weigh in," wait while a ride operator computed a formula for speed based upon the total weight of the passengers, and then pray the operator got his figures right. Luckily for the life expectancy of thrill seekers, the Leap the Gap never went beyond the testing stage.

Other bizarre design proposals followed Meyer's, such as the coaster that would have ducked under a lake in the middle of the ride. Another would have flipped riders around a 360-degree loop, strapped to nothing but roller skates. While the idea of roller skates was abandoned, the idea of tumbling upside down through a loop wasn't.

In 1888 inventor Lina Beecher built America's first looping coaster, the Flip-Flap. He sold his looper to Captain Paul Boyton, a former frogman turned coaster designer, who set the ride up on Coney Island.

What was the ride like? First you and another passenger would climb into the small car. Since seat belts hadn't been invented, you brace yourself by holding onto the sides of the car. The switch is thrown, and you shoot down the thirty-foot-high incline, your fingers growing numb as they dig into the sides of the car. You try to scream, but your stomach squeezes the breath out of your lungs as you hit the bottom of the incline, then whip up, feetfirst, and flip upside down through the loop. You whip out of the loop, jerk to a screeching halt, and sink down in the seat. The ride lasted less than ten seconds, but it was one you would never forget.

At the turn of the century most people had never heard of centrifugal force and were amazed that no one fell out. In fact, so many people paid admission to watch others ride the Flip-Flap that a sign had to be posted warning, "Beware of Pickpockets." But even if people had not been afraid to ride it, the coaster was doomed. A rider went through the loop so fast that he was thrown upside down with the force of 12 G's, which meant he was pushed down into his seat with a strength equaling twelve times his normal body weight. By comparison, astronauts at lift-off experience under 5 G's. After many complaints of neck and back injuries, the Flip-Flap went out of business.

Thirteen years later Edward Prescott built a looping coaster that corrected Beecher's mistakes. To do this, Prescott cleverly hired a respected engineer, E.A. Green. Green designed self-steering cars with rubber wheels and created a sturdy steel loop complete with guard rails. Most important, the loop was fashioned in an ellipse, or teardrop shape, rather than a perfect circle. This meant the passengers entered and exited the loop on a gradually curving course and gravity forces were kept below the danger zone.

Named the Loop-the-Loop, Prescott's coaster cost $400 thousand to build and opened on Coney Island in 1902. Immediately, it attracted national news coverage when a glass of water strapped to a coaster seat went through the loop without spilling a drop!

Engineering feat though it was, Prescott's looping coaster also closed within a short time. His looper did not meet the three rules for any successful amusement ride: a large seating capacity, repeat rides, and a death-defying appearance which, at the same time,

*Spectators watch in amazement as another car whirls around the Flip-Flap*

*The Whirl-Fly is just one of the many bizarre coaster ideas that never went beyond the drawing board.*

seems completely safe to passengers. There was no doubt in riders' minds that the coaster appeared dangerous, but no rider ever believed that the loop was safe. In addition, because of stresses to the loop from the speeding cars, only one four-passenger car could go through the loop at a time. Therefore, not enough passengers could ride the coaster each day to make a profit. Besides, after experiencing one ride on the loop, passengers were not eager to endure an instant replay.

While American coaster designers went through this stage of experimentation, another idea took shape that would bring coasters and other amusement rides into the twentieth century. Since La Marcus Thompson had introduced his Switchback in 1884, Coney Island had become the mecca of amusement rides. Each ride was privately owned and operated. Builders leased a patch of land, set up their roller coaster, and charged admission to ride.

Captain Paul Boyton conceived the novel idea of grouping several rides into a single space and enclosing it with a tall fence. Instead of buying one ticket for each ride, patrons would now pay a single admission fee at the entrance. Thus on July 4, 1895, Captain Boyton opened Sea Lion Park, the world's first all-enclosed amusement park.

Boyton also unveiled a new type of roller coaster. Named the Shoot-the-Chutes, this coaster was the grandfather of modern log rides. If you had been at Sea Lion Park on opening day and ridden the Chutes, you and eleven other passengers would have gone up a steep ramp in a flat-bottomed boat. The boat would pause briefly at the top, giving you just a second to gaze at the ground below. Then it would tip forward and whoosh down a water-filled slide, hitting the bottom with a splashy bounce, to skim across a lagoon.

Boyton operated Sea Lion Park for seven years before he sold it to a couple of clever young men, Frederic Thompson and Elmer Dundy. They tore down the old rides and built a completely new amusement park, which they renamed Luna Park. The men boasted about their revolutionary rides, including a roller coaster named the Mountain Torrent.

In this variation of the Shoot-the-Chutes, passengers could get to the top by either riding up an eighty-foot escalator or climbing a winding path. Two passengers sat in a toboggan-type car with one stretched out in front leaning against the other's chest. Then the car would speed down, around, and through the mountain on a slick water slide. As a bonus, passen-

*A flat-bottom boat splashes across the pool at the Shoot-the-Chutes, while another waits its turn.*

33

gers received a refreshing splash in the face when the car bounced across a pool before stopping.

In order to attract more customers, Thompson and Dundy pulled off a number of innovative publicity stunts. The most successful stunt had live elephants sliding down their own private Shoot-the-Chutes. The elephants seemed to enjoy the ride since they constantly vied to be first in line. Thompson's and Dundy's outrageous gimmick attracted so much attention that many people came to the park just to watch the elephants.

The first true roller coaster to appear at amusement parks during the turn of the century was the Figure-Eight, so named because the track was shaped like the number 8. A chain elevator powered by a steam engine towed the four passenger cars up the lift hill. From that point on, the cars coasted around the track and returned to the station by gravity. The cars were mounted on four castor-type wheels, with a set of "friction wheels" on the side of the cars to guide them over the tracks safely. Brakemen sat in the middle of the train, ready to stop the coaster in any emergency. Since the Figure-Eight glided over gentle dips and curves at a leisurely six miles per hour, the brakemen were known to eat their lunches while riding and were often caught napping on the job.

During the following decades, park owners modified and improved the tracks on Figure-Eights in order to keep up with the larger, faster coasters also being constructed at the time. By 1920 most of the original Figure-Eights either had turned into action-packed rides, or had been torn down to make room for the new thrillers.

Another unusual coaster, named the Cyclone Bowl, appeared at Coney Island in 1910 and is considered by many roller coaster experts to be the most hair-raising ride built during the early part of the century. It was shaped like a large bowl divided by a partition. The ride itself consisted of two sets of spiral tracks, each about one hundred feet in diameter, which tilted up and down. The cars whirled up the tracks of one bowl, then shot over to the other bowl, where they thundered to the bottom. Cyclone Bowls are the rides seen most often in silent movies and old newsreels about Coney Island.

As the coasters became larger and more daring, and coaster stunts grabbed headline space, the names of some coaster builders became household words. Most of these men began their careers building tame Figure-Eights, then progressed to constructing the wilder scream machines. Their names then became linked with the type of coaster that each built.

For example, Frederick Inngersoll was famous for his scenic railways, racing coasters, and Figure-Eights. John Allen of the Philadelphia Tobbogan Company specialized in straight run coasters, rather than those with curves and dips. Allen emphasized both speed and quick shifts from zero to double gravity.

The man considered one of, if not the greatest, roller coaster designer/builder, was John Miller. In 1909 Miller introduced America's first "racing-type coasters." The rides consisted of two separate and very long tracks, down which two coaster cars raced at the same time. With each coaster he built after this, Miller made the lift hills higher, creating steeper drops and more terrifyingly fast rides. Riders loved the bigger coasters, but the increased speed necessitated stricter safety measures. For instance, Miller began fitting his cars with three sets of four wheels.

The first set, attached to the bottoms of the coaster car, carried the weight of the train; the second set, called "side-friction" wheels, were attached to the sides of the car to guide the train along the winding, twisting tracks, keeping it on course. Miller's innovation was a third set, called "undertrack wheels." Undertrack wheels were locked to the car from under the track to prevent the coaster from flying up off the tracks while speeding over the tops of hills. Modernized versions of three sets of wheels are still used today.

Another important safety feature introduced at this time came from an Ohio firm, the Dayton Fun House and Riding Device Manufacturing Company. This company created an automatic lap bar which could only be opened by an attendant with a special key, or by pressing a lever which electronically released the lap bar. Dr. Robert Cartmell, history professor at New York University, and a coaster expert, says, "In my view, roller coasters are among the safest rides at an amusement park, and no more dangerous than a merry-go-round."

As America rolled further into the twentieth century, roller coasters were rolling right along with her. These modern thrill-hills were white-knuckle affairs, that substituted passengers' quiet enjoyment of scenic vistas with sounds that today are practically a ride requirement themselves . . . the sounds of *screams*.

# 4

# Roaring Twenties, Roaring Roller Coasters

If you had grown up during the 1920s you would have searched for uncontrollable speed and reckless excitement. World War I had just ended, the economy was booming, and Americans were ready to "let the good times roll." This carefree attitude inspired people to name this period the "Roaring Twenties." Likewise, as scream machines began plunging one hundred feet on the first drop, flinging passengers around wild and crazy track contortions, the 1920s were named the "Golden Age" of roller coasters.

This Golden Age was brought about in part by the automobile. Automobiles made Americans more mobile, freeing them to move farther away from the trolley lines and the cities. Amusement park owners were quick to note the growth of the suburbs, and soon parks began dotting the American landscape. And since no park would be complete without a roller coaster, designers and builders found themselves

37

*Before a coaster goes into service, it has to be tested for safety. Here sand-bags take the place of humans on the Riverview Park Bobs.*

swamped with orders. As a result, by 1929 almost thirteen hundred scream machines were in existence.

Accompanying this building craze was something even more important—the "Coaster Wars." In order to coax people to drive long distances to an amusement park, designers tried to out-duel each other in the number and intensity of thrills their coasters gave riders. In 1927 two ingenious craftsmen, designer Vernon Keenan and builder Harry Baker, opened the most famous roller coaster in the world—the Coney Island Cyclone.

Your ride on the Cyclone begins with your settling into the seat of your car. Suck in your stomach as an attendant locks the lap bar across your waist. Now the Cyclone starts to climb very slowly up the eighty-three-foot-tall incline. The supports creak and grind. The ramp shakes and rattles and sways. You scream, certain the Cyclone will collapse before you even reach the top of the lift hill!

Finally you're at the top. The Cyclone pauses and you're able to stare over the ramp at the eight steep hills and valleys that await you. Time for a half scream before you pitch forward, the lap bar pushing in your stomach. The plunge forces the breath out of your lungs in a curdling scream. You shoot over a series of hills and valleys at fifty-five miles per hour, whip around a sharp curve, and tear back to the station. Your ride on the Cyclone lasted exactly one minute, forty seconds, but you swear the trip felt more like one hour of screaming, mind-bending terror.

"You're like a cartoon character after being pushed off a ten-story building," said aviation pioneer Orville

Wright following his ride on the Cyclone. "You're in suspended animation." Charles Lindbergh, the first person to fly solo across the Atlantic Ocean commented, "A ride on the Coney Island Cyclone is a greater thrill than flying an airplane at top speed."

Coaster impresario John Allen came the closest to the truth. "Part of the appeal is the imagined danger," he said. "That's why many riders start screaming before the coaster even takes off."

In reality much of the Cyclone's terror comes from the rickety sounds the framework makes as the cars pass over it. What most passengers don't realize is that the sounds were built into the structure on purpose. If the framework was too solid (and therefore quiet), there would be no "give" in the supports as cars thundered over them. After a period of time the constant pressure would weaken the joints, and eventually the entire roller coaster would come crumbling down.

Whether the cause of the terror is real or imagined, the screams produced by the Cyclone are why so many people want to ride it. In at least one case, however, a ride on the Cyclone proved to be therapeutic as well.

This story begins back in January 1943. Emilio Franco, a native of West Virginia, was praying in church when he suddenly keeled over. He came to and appeared to be completely fine except that he had lost his ability to speak. Doctors diagnosed him as having agraphonia, a condition in which speech is lost without organic cause. Unfortunately, his doctors could not cure him. For six years, Franco never uttered a word. Then he took a ride on the Cyclone.

A reporter from the *New York Times* picks up the

*Coney Island's Cyclone plunges down one of its nine giant hills.*

*After being speechless for six years, Emilio Franco took a ride on the Cyclone and was able to mutter, "I feel sick."*

story. "At the second dip Mr. Franco shrieked, grabbed his cousin (who had persuaded him to take the ride) and continued to scream. Throughout the ride his screams were unrestrained. When he landed, his first coherent words since 1943 were: 'I feel sick.' He was sick, but he was also able to talk again!"

Despite such "miracles," the Cyclone had its critics. One writer for *The New Republic* magazine compared coaster cars to "moving coffins." He declared that crowds are battered viciously by these rides, although they are not aware of it, and then asked, "Is this what society wants? Is this what is called 'living dangerously?' Heaven forbid!"

Such criticism didn't stop the crowds from flocking to the Cyclone. It was so popular that it paid off the initial $175 thousand building cost before the first year was out, and is still running strong today.

The public's enthusiasm over the Coney Island Cyclone prompted another coaster builder, Harry Traver, to clone a whole family of them at other amusement parks. Harry Traver, however, unlike Harry Baker and Vernon Keenan, had a reputation for building "extreme machines," tortuous coasters which ignored passengers' safety or comfort. His first Cyclone was built at Crystal Beach Park in Ontario, Canada.

On opening day seventy-five thousand people pushed through the gates and knocked down guard railings just to look at the giant coaster. The innovative feature on this ride was that the lead car started around the first curve *before* the last car in the coaster train even reached the top of the lift hill. Every turn twisted sharply, and there was no let-up in thrills during the entire ride.

*The heart-stopping, terrifying hills look almost gentle in this aerial view of the Riverside Park Cyclone.*

As the Cyclone raced through the figure-eight track at top speed, riders often fainted, and many received broken ribs from being thrown against the person next to them. The Crystal Beach Cyclone was the only known roller coaster to have a registered nurse on duty at all times, and the hot dog stand even sold splints! The Crystal Beach Cyclone was torn down in 1947, but it is still considered the most vicious ride ever built.

Traver inaugurated another Cyclone in 1928 at Palisades Park, New Jersey. "As a connoisseur of roller coasters, I advise you to consult a doctor before you climb aboard the new 'Cyclone,'" wrote a reporter for the *New York Telegram*. "'Cyclone' doesn't play fair. It drags you up an incline, tosses you down the other side, turns you over this way, turns you over that way, and before you can remember what comes after 'Thy Kingdom Come,' shoots you to the stars again."

The Cyclone went to California in 1950 with the appearance of the Cyclone Racer at Long Beach's Pike Amusement Park. For this Cyclone, Harry Traver teamed with coaster designer Frederick Church and built what might appear to be a monster rising out of the sea. The effect was created by having a portion of its track extended over the Pacific Ocean. The visual thrill was accented by the actual ride. You would have screamed at being flung around a sharp curve so close to the ocean that you held your breath in case the Cyclone Racer slipped off the tracks and plunged into the foaming surf below.

Because of the park's short distance from Hollywood, dozens of American motion pictures used the Cyclone Racer as a backdrop. Even the *Beast from*

*Harry Travers made a specialty of building truly terrifying Cyclones known as "extreme machines."*

*Twenty Thousand Fathoms* stomped over the Racer's tracks. Sadly for coaster enthusiasts, the Cyclone Racer was demolished in 1968.

The masterpiece of the Golden Age was another Traver/Church collaboration called the Aeroplane. The Aeroplane opened in 1928 at Playland Amusement Park in Rye Beach, New York, and caught the public's attention immediately. Even the Smithsonian Institution felt compelled to label the Aeroplane, "The greatest body-wringer and most violent roller coaster ride ever built."

The ride began by hauling the cars to the top of an eighty-five-foot lift hill. Then, instead of falling over the drop, the cars reeled around a curve and ducked the feet under the lift hill. From this position the

*The Bobs dives down a steep incline, throwing riders against the sides of their cars.*

Aeroplane dropped into a seventy-four-foot-high "whirlpool," a spiral track banked so steeply that riders were slammed against the sides of their cars. Two-thirds of the way down, the cars accelerated through the ride's legendary "Station House Turn." The turn was made scarier when the seemingly runaway cars tilted on their sides so close to the ground that riders believed the cars would really crash. After the cars pulled out of this initial drop, the remainder of the ride was surprisingly smooth.

Church actually heightened the risk of riding the Aeroplane by not using locking bars to hold passengers in their seats. Instead, he had a stationary bar which riders slid under when climbing into the cars. Church simply didn't feel he had to "build a bubble" around riders. But Church was no fool; he knew riders wanted to know the coaster, no matter how thrilling, was truly safe. To do this, Church inspected the tracks every morning by riding in the first car standing up!

Fred Church admired his creation so much that he accepted a position as ride superintendent of Playland and moved his entire family to New York. The Rye Beach Aeroplane would be the first on a long list of aeroplane coasters, but like many classic Golden Age coasters, it was demolished after its 1957 season.

With the same speed that roller coasters were constructed during the Roaring Twenties, they were demolished after the Great Depression hit in 1929. With millions of Americans unemployed, amusement park attendance declined drastically. Many park owners couldn't afford to maintain their coasters properly or pay for insurance. The problem was accented with the coming of the Second World War and the strict rationing of wood and rubber. Without these materials many existing coasters rotted and became unsafe to operate. New coasters were made of steel but shrank in size to mild-mannered imitations of their scream machine ancestors. It's no wonder that the thirteen hundred roller coasters that existed in 1929 were reduced to just two hundred by the time World War II was over.

Amusement park owners looked forward eagerly to building new and better roller coasters when the war ended. But just as scream machines were once again ready to roar into life, the invention of a thirteen-inch black box knocked the cars off their tracks. Television kept Americans at home on living room sofas, instead of at amusement parks. Fortunately, one man did not give in to the hypnotic power of television. Instead, he waged a one-man battle to rejuvenate the outdoor amusement park industry and with it roller coasters. This man was Walter Elias Disney.

# 5
# Theme Parks and the Roller Coaster Revival

Legend says that one day Walt Disney took his granddaughter to ride the merry-go-round at a local amusement park. When they arrived, Disney was shocked at what he saw. Litter cluttered the grounds, rust corroded the ride cars, and the roller coaster was a rotting, paint-peeling feast for termites.

Walt Disney was saddened by the park's deteriorating condition and asked himself, "Why not build a clean, well-organized amusement park where the entire family can have fun?" Why not?

On June 8, 1955, Disney opened the gates to Disneyland, a $10 million amusement park built on a 180-acre orange grove in Anaheim, California. Disneyland was divided into three separate sections: a "Magic Kingdom," where fantasy reigned; an American folklore section called "Frontier Land" where heroes such as Paul Bunyan and Casey Jones starred; and a "World of Tomorrow," where rides and entertainment were based upon predicted life in the future. Disney's idea of centering the park's different sections around a particular theme was revolutionary in the amusement park industry. Crowds swarmed to Disneyland that opening day and every day since. Disney clearly had a hit on his hands, and "theme parks" were born.

Right away other amusement park owners "went theming." They substituted the word "theme," for "amusement," and entertainment parks were now referred to as "theme parks." Most park owners weren't as ambitious as Disney, preferring to base their parks upon a single theme. For instance, Six Flags Over Texas, which opened in Arlington in 1961, was themed around the six countries to rule Texas before it became a state. Because of the many theme parks that emerged across the United States, each needing at least one roller coaster, but usually showcasing two or three, America's scream machines rolled again in a way that had not been seen since the Roaring Twenties.

In 1959 Disneyland opened its first roller coaster, the Matterhorn. The Matterhorn is a 146-foot-high poured-concrete copy of Switzerland's famed Matterhorn Mountain and uses steel for the tracks. Coaster cars shaped like bobsleds zig-zag down and through the mountain, finishing with a bumpy splash over a small lake.

As successful as the Matterhorn was, it took until 1972 before "Coaster War II" was launched. That was the year John Allen built a giant wooden racing coaster for Cincinnati's King's Island Park. Named the Racer, this coaster rekindled America's love for "woodies" and

*Theme parks saved coasters. Here riders express their joy aboard the Screamin' Eagle roller coaster.*

produced a new generation of wooden scream machines. Among the best known are such monsters as Elitch Gardens's Mr. Twister, in Denver; Cedar Point Park's Gemini, in Sandusky, Ohio; and Magic Mountain's Colossus, in Valencia, California. The Colossus is a megawooden racer in which passengers feel weightless eleven times while speeding forward or backward around its two tracks, each 4,601 feet long.

John Allen did not retire from building woodies because of the competition. He constructed his second wooden monster, the Great American Scream Machine, at Six Flags Over Georgia in Atlanta. Allen followed this with the Rebel Yell, at Kings Dominion Park in Doswell, Virginia, in 1975; the Thunder Road at Carowinds Park in Charlotte, North Carolina, in 1976; and in 1975–76, his Screamin' Eagle at Six Flags Over Mid-America, near St. Louis. The Screamin' Eagle rose 110 feet above the ground and set the record for the highest roller coaster in the world.

The number of wooden coasters might have continued to rise if the price of wood and the labor costs for constructing the intricate frameworks had not skyrocketed. Many coaster builders were forced to switch to steel. But instead of the small, tame "steelies," the designers now created true scream machines by using steel to build tubular tracks. Tubular steel tracks allowed for more flexibility and let designers do something which had been tried since the close of the nineteenth century—turn riders upside down.

The United States' first modern loop-the-loop, the Corkscrew, was built in 1976 at Knotts' Berry Farm theme park in Buena Park, California. After an opening drop of 70 feet, the Corkscrew speeds around a sharp curve. As the train hits forty-three miles per hour, the Corkscrew flips upside down through two barrel rolls.

By 1980 some variations of the Corkscrew had been invented. One coaster design company added two reverse points, or dead-end hills. On a shuttle loop, riders are catapulted forward and backward through a 61-foot-high vertical loop and endure near plunges off two 140 foot high, dead-end hills.

The second variation of the Corkscrew is the vertical 360-degree loop, which flips riders completely upside down. Spin-offs of the vertical loop are the double loop roller coaster, the triple loop, and finally, a quintuple loop found on the Viper at Connecticut's Darien Lake Park.

When ride inventors exhausted the upside-down track layout, they came up with another way to scare people senseless. They switched tracks on the riders! Instead of having cars travel over the tracks, the cars were hung from overhead tracks, and the "suspended coaster" was created. The first successful suspended roller coaster was designed by the Arrow/Huss Corporation in 1984 for Busch Gardens, The Old Country, in Williamsburg, Virginia. If you're not afraid, hop aboard the Big Bad Wolf!

A wolf howls, its cries piercing the woods ahead. You cringe, locked into your coaster car, hanging suspended off the ground. You pitch forward.

Your heart pounds furiously as the Wolf swings you to the right, to the left, silently plunging you down a water-filled ravine, practically dunking you. In the

*Two cars racing over a "small" hill on the Colossus.*

Magic Mountain Park, CA

*The Corkscrew spins through a second loop at 45 miles per hour.*

middle of the ride the Wolf springs up the lift hill, hurtling you down, toward a Bavarian village. Look out! That cabin's flying straight at you! The Wolf hairpins left, barely missing another cabin.

Is the ride over? No. The Wolf stalks up a second lift hill. It jackknifes toward the ravine, then rears its head and shoots through two water jets at 48 miles per hour. Before you can blink the spray from your eyes, the animal darts back to the Wolf's den. You sink into your seat, your pulse pounding. You have just survived a howling ride on the Big Bad Wolf!

With looping and suspended coasters leading the way of space age scream machines, what next? Kings Island Amusement Park in Kings Mill, Ohio, gave the world an answer with their 1984 coaster invention, the King Cobra.

The "snake" slithers up a ninety-five-foot-high incline, tumbles downhill at fifty miles per hour, and coils through a 360-degree loop. Snaking out of the loop, the Cobra curls around a 540-degree spiral turn over a lake, sidewinds over camelback hills until, after two minutes of serpentine thrills, the King Cobra hisses back into the station.

So what's so new about the Cobra? When the shoulder harness is released, you don't have to stand up to climb out of the coaster car. You're already standing! The King Cobra is America's first "stand-up" roller coaster. Riders stand in twenty-four passenger trains, strapped in by an arm harness with a lap bar across their stomachs, while slithering around the 2,010-foot track.

"It's like skiing fifty miles per hour down a slope," said one passenger. A teenaged girl commented, "I felt like I was flying through the air, like my body wasn't hooked to anything."

With the unleashing of the Big Bad Wolf, and the King Cobra, you might think roller coasters have reached the limits of mind-bending terror on tracks. Yet at a recent "Ultimate Roller Coaster" competition, three test pilots submitted the KC-135, a ride designed to help astronauts learn to function while weightless.

*Swinging out on the Big Bad Wolf.*

Busch Gardens, The Dark Continent, FL

61

The test pilots described the ride. "Start at twenty-five thousand feet, peak at thirty-five thousand feet, then fly across nine miles of track in seventy seconds." The KC-135 unanimously won the competition and came away with an appropriate nickname—the "Vomit Comet."

# 6

# Space Age
# Scream Machines

"We knew so little about engineering . . ." admitted Joseph McKee, prominent turn-of-the-century coaster designer. "In 1905 when I started building roller coasters, they were really just a long, gentle coast out and back, with a few dips and curves thrown in for variety."

Back then, designers didn't think about things like pulling G's, centrifugal forces or weightlessness. They weren't aware that these forces played a significant role in how your coaster behaved, much less that they affected the riders.

Today, however, roller coaster builders must master the same engineering and computer skills as the people who build rockets. In fact it takes a team of highly trained engineers—industrial, structural, hydraulic, mechanical, and electrical—to design a modern coaster.

For instance, the team begins the creation of a new

63

*It took a team of highly skilled engineers to design the Mind Bender, the world's only triple loop coaster.*

coaster by consulting physicians about the biomechanics of the ride. If too many positive gravity forces push riders down in their seats, back and neck injuries may result. And if overly powerful negative gravity forces lift riders out of their seats, the lap bar or shoulder harness might not be strong enough to keep riders from falling out.

What exactly is a gravity force? A gravity force, usually referred to as a G, is any change in gravity which causes a change in your weight. One G Unit (1 G) is what you weigh standing still. Each time you move, your weight changes. The force which changes your weight is called inertia. Once you are moving in one direction, inertia will make your body resist any force that tries to change that direction. For instance, as you plunge down one hill on a roller coaster, then speed up the next, inertia resists this upward direction change by pulling you down into your seat. This downward pushing also creates the centrifugal force that keeps you in your seat when flipping upside down. Centrifugal force works so long as a constant speed is maintained. In fact, while tumbling through a loop, the shoulder harness is only necessary if the car should slow down for any reason.

How many gravity forces you "pull" depends upon how much you weigh. For example, if you weigh one hundred pounds and pull three extra gravity forces, 3 G's, you will weigh three times that, or three hundred pounds.

Sometimes inertia creates gravity forces which make you weigh less. When you race up the lift hill, go over the top, and speed downhill, inertia resists the downward change in direction and keeps pushing you up. You are lifted out of your seat. You are now carrying less than your normal weight. Sometimes, like astronauts floating in space, a ride on a roller coaster can take away all the gravity forces working on your body, and you will be totally weightless. When you tear out of a 360-degree loop, dart up a dead-end hill, and stop, inertia resists both the uphill change in direction from speeding down the loop curve, and the direction change from speeding uphill to the sudden stop. Now inertia pulls you up with stronger gravity forces than are pulling you down, thus taking away all your body weight, and you become weightless.

Once gravity forces have been considered, engineers draw up a preliminary blueprint of the roller coaster. Design engineers feed information into a computer, including the dimension of each section of track, to see if both positive and negative gravity forces are safe. If the computer calculates G forces that are not safe for riders, the engineer makes changes in the track layout.

Next, other engineers take aerial photographs of the construction site. These photographs show obstacles which might be in the way of the roller coaster, such as trees, lakes, and ditches. Whenever possible, builders try to use a park's natural environment to enhance their rides, rather than destroy the land. When Arrow/Huss Corporation built the Loch Ness Monster at Busch Gardens in Williamsburg, Virginia, engineers felt the lake and the forestlike surroundings would produce a sensational effect. Against the roller coaster's bright yellow tracks and the dark support beams that blend into the scenery, the "mon-

*The Kennywood Thunderbolt shows how a coaster is often designed to fit into a park's natural environment.*

ster" would look like a yellow giant towering above the trees.

From all this information two types of blueprints are drawn for each roller coaster. One looks like a blueprint for a house. The other, called a vertical profile, looks as if the engineer has taken his pencil and drawn a bunch of straight lines across the paper. The lines represent the scaled down dimensions of each section of track. To show the loops, turns, and other "big events" of the ride, the engineer marks an X across the lines at the points in the track where they occur.

*The Loch Ness Monster roars into a loop. Note the way the track has bee[n] fitted into the landscape.*

A member of the team uses the vertical profile as a road-map to stake out the ride. A stake is driven into the ground at each point in the ride where a "big event" occurs. This allows the construction team to see whether a lift hill or a curve in the track is planned too close to water pipes, telephone poles, or some other stationary object.

For instance, when the Loch Ness Monster was staked out, designers discovered an underground gas pipeline located where the middle of the ride was planned. Holes could not be dug here for the concrete footings which hold the support columns. Structural engineers solved the problem by designing a bridge with "kickers," or side supports, extending from the bridge.

Once the stakeout is completed, roller coaster construction becomes a matter of mathematics. Engineers compute the two unknowns in roller coaster design—the speed of the cars and the time it takes to lose this speed. After the cars are dragged up the lift hill and take the first plunge, they run by gravity alone. If the speed is not fast enough at the beginning of the ride, the gravity will be used up and the cars will stop before they return to the loading station. On the other hand, if the coaster drops down the lift hill too fast, gravity will propel the cars so fast that the brakes cannot stop the train without jolting the passengers. If a change in the speed is necessary, engineers merely change the height of the lift hill.

The track is manufactured at the factory in sections, then shipped to the amusement park. At the building site, concrete footings are poured and a crane lifts the support columns into place. For the Loch Ness

Monster, 136 columns, each 30 inches in diameter, were used to support the ride's 3,300 feet of track.

Next workers attach the track to the support columns. Laying a roller coaster track is like building a model airplane. Just as you make sure the airplane parts fit together perfectly before applying the glue, so track layers must fit each section of track together before welding them together. A flaw of as little as one-eighth of an inch off will cause the cars to bump over this section.

When the track is laid, the power-operated drag pulley to haul the cars up the lift hill is installed. Then the coaster cars, which have also been manufactured at the factory and shipped to the park, are rolled onto the loading platform. Now the coaster is given a test run without any passengers, called an "empty run." If the roller coaster makes it around the tracks without any problems, the engineers receive a bonus for their months of hard work—they get to ride it!

If you feel brave enough, you can join them on a test run of the Loch Ness Monster.

You're sitting thirteen stories above a lake, when the Monster shoves you 114 feet downhill, hurtling from twelve to sixty miles per hour in two and one-half seconds. The speed produces a monstrous, 3.5 G takeoff. Now you're curling through one of the Monster's two interlocking, 360-degree loops when all of a sudden another coaster races toward you. You are about to crash when the invading Monster pulls up onto the interlocking loop and tosses upside down above your head.

When you recover from this encounter you realize you're heading for the Monster's Lair. Catapulted into

*The twisting steel tracks are checked daily for stress cracks, loose fittings, and weird noises.*

the dark tunnel, you spin around and around, two and three-quarter times in eighteen seconds. You feel the force of 1.5 G's pulling you down. Twisting, turning, spiraling, spinning, you blast out of the Lair to freedom, having conquered the two minutes and ten seconds of the Loch Ness Monster!

The completion of the roller coaster is only the beginning of work on the scream machine. Safety checks will continue for the rest of the coaster's life. Each day before the amusement park opens, mechanical engineers "walk the track," hiking over every foot to check for loose or missing bolts. They also retrieve any possessions lost by passengers, such as scarves, hats, and candy wrappers. Obstacles on the track can catch in the coaster's wheels and slow down the pro-grammed speed.

As a double safeguard, at least once a week opera-tors and maintenance workers take a marathon ride on the coaster. Their ears are trained to hear unusual clanking, which means something is loose on a sec-tion of track. If the engineers hear such noises, the roller coaster is shut down until the problem is found and repaired.

One of the latest safety measures is the electronic block system. The track is divided up into blocks, or sections, designated by computer. Each coaster car is equipped with computerized, photocell and magnetic sensors. These sensors permit only one train at a time to go through a block. If the first train stops for any reason, the sensors automatically stop the second be-fore a crash happens.

So it is that while winter has been turning into spring, pieces of steel have been turning into a solid and safe Screamin' Demon, Shock Wave, or Mind Bender. And when summer officially arrives, amuse-ment parks across the United States will unleash their newest, fastest, fiercest scream machines.

# 7

# *Coaster Encounters Across America*

On August 18, 1977, Richard Rodriguez, a nine-teen-year-old college student, climbed aboard the Coney Island Cyclone to celebrate that roller coaster's fiftieth birthday. Four days later Rodriguez finished celebrating.

Rodriguez had ridden the cyclone for 103 hours and 55 minutes, or 2,361 straight rides. He had set a scream machine riding record, and a new sport, roller coaster marathoning, was born. Within a year Richard Rodriguez went on to conquer coasters across the United States, including Myrtle Beach Park's Swamp Fox for 110 hours, and the Rebel Yell at Kings Dominion Park, Virginia, for 124 hours.

Following Rodriguez's headline-making rides, other individuals joined the marathoning circuit, and soon records were falling almost as quickly as they were made. In July of 1980, Jim King, a very serious coaster lover, won the wooden marathoning record for enduring the Starliner at Miracle Strip Park in Panama City, Florida, for 368 hours, or 15 days and 8 hours straight. Carl Eichelman, a forty-three-year-old Internal Revenue Service supervisor by night and a roller coaster rider by day, holds the world's record for riding the Beast at King's Island Park in Cincinnati 4,022 times during a five-year period.

If you wanted to make a marathon ride, you would first obtain permission from the amusement park director where the roller coaster was located. Then you would arrange for some friends to "spot" you throughout the run. This crew would be responsible for keeping the breaking area of the track dry, including mopping up after a rainfall. They would also supply you with hot dogs, popcorn, and other nourishment as you zipped through the loading station.

Next you would take months getting in shape. Richard Rodriguez spent hundreds of hours on playground swings, building up his tolerance to the continual ups and downs of the roller coaster. On the day of your marathon, you would pack both warm and cold weather clothes, suntan lotions and ski masks for protection against windburn, and a pillow and blanket for sleeping. Amazingly, some marathoners really do fall asleep.

Official marathon rules are few and simple. You are allowed one five-minute break every hour, or you may accumulate up to twenty minutes of break time by riding nonstop for four hours. That way, you can stretch your legs and visit the restroom.

Where's the best place to sit while marathoning? Most likely you would sit in the middle cars where G forces are not so strong. For more of that "floating on air" sensation, sit in the first seats. The back seats will give you a body-wringing ride. As you pitch over a hill, the car seems to lift right off the tracks. The last seat is best on a shuttle loop roller coaster. When you fly up backward, you'll be suspended the highest of all the coaster cars, and totally weightless.

Once on the coaster, you would have the company of other paying customers during the day. At night you would be on your own, with only the ride attendant and one of your crew for company. You might try to amuse yourself by attaching a tape player to your coaster car. One marathoner learned how to speak Spanish by listening to tapes of Spanish lessons during his ride.

What else is there to do during the hours of zooming around a track? You could work to heighten the sensations of the ride.

For more of a feeling of weightlessness, lift your feet up as you go over a hill. When riding in one of the rear cars, lift your feet and look up. This is particularly wonderful when the coaster dives downhill. You will see the support structure fly up and away from you, creating a feeling much like free-falling through space.

When tossing upside down through a loop, turn your head from right to left. The sky will rotate, and you will get extra upside-down dizzies. And for a really scary ride, keep your eyes closed.

The national attention paid marathoners, as well as the opening of new and ever more exciting scream machines has created thousands of coaster lovers. In addition, a roller coaster organization has been formed named the American Coaster Enthusiasts (ACE). ACE lets coaster buffs compare historical notes, share stories of rides on different roller coasters, and keep each other informed about new coasters on the horizon. ACE is headquartered in Chicago and at present has over one thousand members from both America and Europe.

What does the future hold in store for these and other coaster enthusiasts? Some will insist that the future has arrived in the form of two space age coasters that opened in 1985.

The first is the Z Force, located at Six Flags Great America amusement park in Illinois. The Z Force consists of a track layout in the shape of a pyramid of "Z's." The four-car trains, each holding four passengers seated side by side, zig-zags up the Z, then nose-dives into the six vertical Z-shaped turns. The constant change of speed, combined with the Z-motion, creates a sensation never before experienced. Said one daredevil, "It's that cloud nine sense of flight."

The second is Dragon Mountain, North America's highest (186 feet) steel roller coaster, and the world's largest and longest steel machine with 5,500 feet of track. The Dragon cost $10 million to build and is located at Marineland Park in Niagara Falls, Canada.

An initial plunge down a 186-foot drop begins the frolic. Then the Dragon dashes up and around two vertical loops, roars into a double horizontal spiral turn inside a volcano, complete with artificial flowing lava and a lifesize animated dragon. Zooming out of the volcano, the Dragon swoops behind a one-third size reproduction of Niagara's Canadian Falls, enters into another tunnel in front of the American Falls, and

*The Z Force dives down one of its six vertical turns.*

ducks into a third, completely dark, twisting tunnel. Shooting out the tunnel's mouth, riders are unable to see the upcoming adventure until their cars are already flipping through it—a double-barrel roll around two vertical loops shaped like a "bow-tie." The ride is one wild track contortion after another and lasts an incredible jam-packed 3.2 minutes.

Can anything new and exciting ever top a ride on Dragon Mountain? Ron Toomer, design engineer for Arrow/Huss Corporation, thinks so. "In the future, we'll probably see even more features analogous to big performance aircraft." Recently Toomer invented the "boomerang" turn. Within the space of thirteen seconds, the coaster enters a kidney-shaped, double-barrel-roll track section, flipping upside down twice, before blasting out the same way it roared in. The boomerang was first endured on the Orient Express roller coaster at Worlds of Fun Amusement Park in Kansas City, Missouri.

Paul Ruben, a roller coaster historian, believes that people will not be satisfied with riding roller coasters which merely leap and flip into wild track contortions. He believes future roller coasters will become space age versions of La Marcus Thompson's scenic railways of a century ago, featuring animated audio and visual effects, such as Dragon Mountain's "erupting volcano."

As your roller coaster ride through the centuries pulls to a halt, you look over your shoulder to where you have been—from Russia's ice slides to scenic railways, Leap the Gaps, and Cyclones. Around you in the present are the Z Forces, the King Cobras and Dragon Mountains. Then you try to peer into the future, wondering what roller coaster thrills are yet to come. Rest easy, for just like their predecessors, today's design engineers are at work. Even while you read this they are thinking, imagining and drawing up plans for the "ultimate" roller coaster. The question is, will you be ready to ride it?

*Scream Machines are engineering marvels with a long, proud history. But even more important, they're terrific fun to ride!*

# *A List of America's Best Roller Coasters*

## California

**Disneyland,** 1313 Harbor Blvd., Anaheim, California 92803

SPACE MOUNTAIN, 1977. Indoor coaster. 2 minutes 40 seconds. This coaster rolls inside a darkened building accompanied by light and sound show featuring speeding rockets.

MATTERHORN, 1959. Steel. 2 minutes. One of the earliest steel coasters with toboggan-style cars.

**Knotts' Berry Farm,** 8039 Beach Blvd., Buena Park, California 90620

CORKSCREW, 1975. Looper. H. 75 ft., L. 1,250 ft.; 1 minute 10 seconds. The first successful looping coaster in America.

MONTEZUMA'S REVENGE, 1978. Shuttle loop. H. 140 ft., L. 850 ft.; 37 seconds. Travels forward and backward through a vertical loop.

**Santa Cruz Beach Boardwalk,** 400 Beach St., Santa Cruz, California 95061

GIANT DIPPER, 1924. Wooden twister. H. 75 ft., L. 2,640 ft.; 2 minutes. "Dip" is an understatement as this roller coaster immediately nose-dives out of the loading station into a tunnel.

# Colorado

**Elitch's Gardens,** 4620 West 38th Ave., Denver, Colorado 80212

MR. TWISTER, 1964. Wooden twister. H. 95 ft., L. 3,020 ft.; 2 minutes. Mr. Twister performs incredible acrobatics, coupled with an uncanny ability to surprise you.

**Lakeside Amusement Park,** 4601 Sheridan Blvd., Denver, Colorado 80212

CYCLONE, 1940. Wooden out and back. H. 90 ft., L. 2,800 ft.; 2 minutes 15 seconds. The art deco motif is especially striking.

# Florida

**Walt Disney World,** Lake Buena Vista, Florida 32830

SPACE MOUNTAIN, 1976. Indoor. The double of the indoor roller coaster at Disneyland.

**Busch Gardens,** The Dark Continent, 3000 Busch Blvd., Tampa, Florida 33612

**PYTHON,** 1976. Looper. H. 70 ft., L. 1,250 ft.; 1 minute 10 seconds. The second barrel-rolling coaster in the United States.

# Georgia

**Six Flags Over Georgia,** Route I-20, Atlanta, Georgia 30336

**GREAT AMERICAN SCREAM MACHINE,** 1972–73. Wooden. H. 105 ft., L. 3,800 ft.; 1 minute 40 seconds. Built around a lake, this is one of the most beautiful roller coasters in the country.

**MIND BENDER,** 1978. Triple looper. H. 130 ft., L. 3,235 ft.; 1 minute 50 seconds. Performs three front flips.

# Illinois

**Six Flags Great America,** Interstate 94 at Exit 132, Gurnee, Illinois 60031

**TURN OF THE CENTURY,** 1976. Looper. H. 95 ft., L. 2,190 ft.; 1 minute 45 seconds.

**TIDAL WAVE,** 1978. Shuttle loop. H. 142 ft., L. 849 ft.; 37 seconds.

**THE DEMON,** 1980. Loop. H. 100 ft., L. 1,250 ft.; 1 minute 45 seconds. Features a one hundred-foot drop toward a wall of boulders.

# Iowa

**Adventureland,** Interstate 80 and Route 65, Altoona, Iowa 50316

**TORNADO,** 1978. Wooden out and back. H. 93 ft., L. 3,280 ft.; 2 minutes. Takes the scenic route around a lake.

# Massachusetts

**Riverside Park,** Main Street, Agawam, Massachusetts 01001

**THUNDERBOLT,** 1940. Wooden. H. 68 ft., L. 2,865 ft.; 57 seconds. The speed of 37 MPH seems very much faster.

**Paragon Park,** 175 Nantasket Ave., Hull, Massachusetts 02005

**GIANT COASTER,** 1917. Wooden. H. 98 ft., L. 3,300 ft.; 1 minute 50 seconds. One of the few remaining Golden Age coasters, and an enduring favorite of coaster fans.

# Missouri

**Six Flags Over Mid-America,** Route I-44, Eureka, Missouri 63025

**SCREAMIN' EAGLE,** 1975. Wooden out and back. H. 110 ft., L. 3,872 ft.; 2 minutes 30 seconds. The third-ranked biggest roller coaster in the world, and is noted for a ninety-two-foot drop in the *third* hill.

**RIVER KING MINE RIDE,** 1971. Wooden mine ride. L. 2,349 ft.; 3 minutes. An exciting trip for the younger coaster fan.

# New Jersey

**Six Flags, Great Adventure,** N.J. Turnpike (Exit 7A) and Route I-95, Jackson, New Jersey 08527

**LIGHTNIN' LOOPS,** 1978. Shuttle loop. Upper loop, H. 85 ft., lower loop, H. 62 ft.; L. 635 ft. Two separate roller coasters race through interlocking shuttle loops.

**ROLLING THUNDER,** 1979. Racer. H. 88 ft., L. 3,200 ft.; 2 minutes. Racing coasters alternate hills and valleys after the first drop instead of speeding side by side.

# New York

**Astroland Coney Island,** Surf at 10th St., Brooklyn, New York 11232

**CYCLONE,** 1927. Wooden twister. H. 85 ft., L. 2,640 ft.; 1 minute 40 seconds. The most famous roller coaster in the world, with a 60-degree first drop called the steepest of any roller coaster operating today.

**THUNDERBOLT,** 1925. Wooden twister. H. 86 ft.; 1 minute 17 seconds. A Golden Age coaster built over the old Kensington Hotel.

**Rockaway Playland Park,** Rockaway Beach, 185 Beach 97th St., Queens, New York 11693

**COASTER,** 1938. Wooden. H. 70 ft., L. 3,030 ft.; 2 minutes. Originally named the Atom Smasher, starred in the motion picture *This Is Cinerama.*

**Westchester County Playland,** Playland Park, Rye, New York 10580

**DRAGON COASTER,** 1929. Wooden. H. 82 ft., L. 3,400 ft.; 2 minutes 4 seconds. Zoom into the Dragon's "fire-breathing" mouth.

# North Carolina

**Carowinds Park,** Route I-77, Charlotte, North Carolina 28210

**THUNDER ROAD,** 1976. Racer. H. 91 ft. 8 in., L. 3,819 ft.; 2 minutes 10 seconds. Coaster cars look like old-fashioned jalopies and hit speeds of 57.75 MPH.

**WHITE LIGHTNIN',** 1977. Shuttle loop. H. 138 ft. 3 in., L. 580 ft.; 35 seconds. Races through a 76.2-foot-high loop at 53 MPH.

**SCOOBY DOO,** 1976. Wooden. H. 40 ft., L. 1,356 ft.; 1 minute 30 seconds. A roller coaster for juniors.

# Ohio

**Kings Island Park,** Route I-71, Kings Mill, Ohio 45034

**THE BEAST,** 1979. Wooden. H. 105 ft., L. 7,400 ft.; 3 minutes 40 seconds. With speeds of 70 MPH this ranks as the number-one scream machine in the world.

**RACER,** 1972. Racing coaster. H. 88 ft., L. 3,415 ft.; 2 minutes 30 seconds. Marked the rebirth of a boom in American wooden coaster construction.

**SCREAMIN' DEMON,** 1978. Looper. H. 56 ft., L. 635 ft. As you flip upside down, you are fifty-eight feet high above a lake.

**Cedar Point Park,** Routes 250, 6, and 2; Ohio Turnpike Exit 7, Sandusky, Ohio 44870

**GEMINI,** 1978. Wooden. H. 125 ft., L. 3,935 ft.; 2 minutes 20 seconds. The 55-degree, 118-foot first drop is a unique thrill.

**BLUE STREAK,** 1964. Wooden out and back. H. 78 ft., L. 2,558 ft.; 1 minute 45 seconds. A typical John Allen "woodie," with the emphasis on smooth speed.

**CEDAR CREEK MINE RIDE,** Corkscrew and The Jumbo Jet, 1970s.

# Pennsylvania

**Lakemont Park,** 118 6th St. at Lakemont, Altoona, Pennsylvania 16602

**LEAP-THE-DIPS,** 1894. Wooden figure eight. H. 48 ft., L. 1,980 ft.; 1 minute. The last remaining wooden roller coaster built before the turn of the century, with gentle slopes and 15 MPH speed.

**Conneaut Lake Park,** Route 79 and 618, Conneaut, Pennsylvania 16316

**BLUE STREAK,** 1937–38. Wooden out and back. H. 79 ft., 10 in., L. 1,900 ft.; 2 minutes 5 seconds.

**Kennywood Park,** 4800 Kennywood Blvd., West Mifflin, Pennsylvania 15122

You can take a ride back to roller coasters' Golden Age, on the Thunderbolt, Jack Rabbit, and Racer, or soar 360 degrees in the Laser Loop.

## South Carolina

**Grand Strand Amusement Park,** 408 South Ocean Blvd., Myrtle Beach, South Carolina 29577

**SWAMP FOX,** 1966. Wooden. H. 75 ft., L. 2,640 ft.

## Texas

**Astroworld,** 9001 Kirby Dr., Houston, Texas 77001

**TEXAS CYCLONE,** 1976. Wooden. H. 92 ft., L. 3,120 ft.; 2 minutes. A mirror image of Coney Island's Cyclone, only bigger.

**GREEZED LIGHTNIN',** 1978. Shuttle loop. H. 138 ft., L. 849 ft.; 33 seconds. The only shuttle loop in the southwestern United States, which many fans claim is the most terrifying ride of all.

**Six Flags Over Texas,** Dallas/Ft. Worth Turnpike, Arlington, Texas 76010

SHOCK WAVE, 1978. Double loop. H. 116 ft., L. 3,500 ft.; 1 minute 58 seconds. Sports two seventy-foot-high loops.

## Virginia

**Busch Gardens,** The Old Country, Highway 60 East, Williamsburg, Virginia 23185

LOCH NESS MONSTER, 1978. Interlocking loops. H. 130 ft., L. 3,240 ft.; 2 minutes 30 seconds. A true "heart-in-your-stomach" coaster since the first drop is a dizzying 114 feet at a 55- degree angle.

## For further information about roller coasters, write to:

**The American Coaster Enthusiasts**
c/o Public Relations Director
Box 8226
Chicago, Illinois 60680

**International Association of Amusement Parks**
Chicago, Illinois 60640

# *Index*